Talking About

Domestic Violence

Nicola Edwards

Chrysalis Children's Books

First published in the UK in 2003 by
Chrysalis Children's Books
An imprint of Chrysalis Books Group Plc
The Chrysalis Building
Bramley Road
London W10 6SP

Paperback edition first published in 2005

ISBN 184138 827 0 (hb)
ISBN 184458 316 3 (pb)

British Library Cataloguing in Publication Data for this book is available from the British Library.

Editorial manager: Joyce Bentley
Senior editor: Sarah Nunn
Picture researchers: Terry Forshaw, Lois Charlton
Designer: Wladek Szechter
Editor: Kate Phelps
Consultant: Dr Ute Navidi, Head of Policy, ChildLine

Printed in China

The pictures used in this book do not show the actual people named in the text.

Foreword

Home is where everyone is supposed to be safe. So witnessing an adult hitting or threatening their partner affects children deeply and can leave life-long emotional scars. Children too may be physically hurt. Frightened, worried sick, ashamed that it's happening to their mum or dad and confused by the abuse of a parent they love, some withdraw into a cloak of silence to protect the family.

Talking About Domestic Violence helps lift this cloak of silence. Sharing this book can help adults and children talk about their anger and pain. It reassures children that violence at home is a crime for which the perpetrator – and never themselves – bears responsibility and provides basic advice about how to cope. Daring to speak out and identifying someone who will listen – a trusted adult, a friend of their own age or ChildLine – means taking the first step towards finding help.

Informative and thought-provoking, the **Talking About** series tackles some disturbing aspects of contemporary society: domestic violence, racism, divorce, eating problems and bullying. Adults often try to protect children from these problems or believe they will not understand. Taking children through a series of situations they can identify with – using words and images – also means offering alternative ways of resolving conflict. Each book shows that even very young children are not passive observers or victims but want to make sense of their world and act to make life better for themselves, their families and other children.

Ute Navidi, Head of Policy, ChildLine

Contents

What is domestic violence?

Domestic violence affects a lot of families in the world today. It happens in the home when a grown-up attacks another adult in the family.

This man is behaving violently to his wife.

Victims of domestic violence often lose **confidence** in themselves.

Domestic violence can go on for years and years.

Hurting someone at home by kicking or hitting them is domestic violence. So is **threatening** to hurt them or saying things to make them feel frightened or small.

Where does it happen?

People usually think of home as a safe place, where they can live happily without any fear.

When violence happens at home, it makes people feel scared.

Peter was frightened when he heard his dad shouting at his mum in the next room.

When someone at home is violent it makes the other members of the family feel unsafe and afraid. They may feel **ashamed** that the violence is happening and wish that their family was more like other people's. They may try to keep the violence a secret.

Who does it?

Most cases of domestic violence involve men attacking women. Men who seem charming and polite to others can be violent at home.

Some women behave violently towards their partners.

When attacks happen over and over again, they can make a family feel worn out, sad and worthless.

Domestic violence happens all over the world, in all kinds of homes, rich and poor. Usually children are at home when the violence is happening – sometimes they are even in the same room.

A repeating pattern?

Some people think that children who see violence at home become used to it. Then, when they grow up, they will behave violently too.

In most families people talk to each other and discuss any disagreements.

When someone becomes violent they lose their **self control**. They don't think about how anyone else is feeling.

In fact, most children who grow up in violent homes do all they can to avoid violence in their adult lives.

Children can leave violent backgrounds behind them and grow into happy adults.

Sad and scared

When someone is violent at home, it is very worrying and frightening for the children. They may feel they cannot talk to their mum or dad about what is happening.

It can be terrifying to experience violence at home.

Greta couldn't sleep when her dad was violent at home.

Sometimes children are attacked, as well as their mother or father.

Children often think that their mum or dad has enough to cope with and do not want to upset them any further.

Worried sick

Children often worry that they must have done something to cause the violence at home. But domestic violence is a **crime** that hurts people and makes them live in fear.

Charlotte was so worried when her step-dad hit her mum that she started having tummy aches.

Toni tried to comfort her little brother. When he was upset, he sometimes wet the bed.

It makes children worry more if adults try to pretend nothing is wrong.

Domestic violence is only ever the fault of the person who is being violent – no one else is to blame.

Feeling angry

No one wants their home to be a violent place. Sometimes it makes children angry that there is violence at home.

David showed he was angry by the way he behaved.

Gina felt angry with her mum for being a victim of domestic violence.

For some children, it seems so unfair that other children's houses are safe and happy places when theirs isn't. They may even blame the person who is being attacked for not being able to stop the violence.

Feeling ashamed

Children can feel ashamed when there is violence at home. They may think that they are the only family in which violence is happening.

Violence at home made it difficult for Mel to **concentrate** at school.

Zoe's aunt listened carefully when Zoe told her she was worried about things at home.

Children can feel very alone, thinking that their friends will not understand what they are going through.

If you are worried about violence at home, talk to an adult you **trust** about it.

Wanting it to stop

It is mostly women who are attacked in the home. Sometimes children try to protect their mothers from attack. This is dangerous, as they can get hurt.

William shouted at his dad to leave his mum alone.

Isabelle phoned the police when she heard her mum being attacked.

Many mothers draw strength from their children. They say that their children made them feel brave enough to escape from a violent home.

Deciding to leave

Often a mum and her children have to leave the family home in a hurry. They might only be able to take a few things with them.

When Ella and Amy left home with their mum, they went to stay with their grandparents.

Mums and children need a place to stay where they will be safe from the person who has been violent towards them.

A **refuge** is a secret house where people escaping from domestic violence can stay.

Children living at a refuge often feel scared but relieved to have left the violence behind.

Separate lives

Leaving a violent home gives mums and their children a chance to build a new life together.

Charlotte was excited when she and her mum left the refuge and moved into a flat of their own.

Jade felt sad because she missed her dad,
even though he'd had to leave home
because he'd been violent.

Families may have to cope with changes
such as a move to a new area. The children
may have to go to a different school and
make new friends.

Leave us alone!

Children whose dad has been violent to them or their mum may not want to see him again. They may be frightened of him and feel they cannot trust him any more.

Jason's dad was only allowed to see him at a special centre where staff could watch his behaviour.

Francesca didn't want to see her dad. She was scared of him.

Children may be worried that their dad will be violent again, even if he says he is sorry and tells them he loves them.

A happier future

It takes time for people who have been hurt and scared by violence to feel safe and happy again. But people do rebuild their lives.

Freya drew pictures to show how she was feeling. After a while she started to draw happy pictures again.

Rachel, Becca and Susie were happy to see their mum laughing again.

There are lots of people who can help them to put the fear and pain of the past behind them. Then they can look forward to a happier future.

Words to remember

ashamed Feeling bad, as if you have done something wrong.

concentrate To give something your full attention.

confidence A feeling that you can do anything.

crime Breaking the laws or rules of a country.

refuge A secret house where people escaping from domestic violence can stay.

self control Being in charge of your feelings.

threatening Telling someone that something bad will happen to them unless, for example, they do what someone else wants.

trust Feeling that someone won't let you down.

Organisations, helplines and websites

FOR CHILDREN:
The police
To contact the police in an emergency dial 999.

ChildLine
A charity offering information, help and advice to any child with worries or problems.
Address for adults:
45 Folgate Street, London E1 6GL
Address for children:
Freepost NATN1111, London E1 6BR
Free and confidential helpline for children and young people: 0800 1111
ChildLine Scotland bullying helpline:
0800 441111
www.childline.org.uk

Refuge
A 24-hour national domestic violence helpline.
2–8 Maltravers Street, London WC2R 3EE
Helpline: 0870 5995443

Samaritans
A 24-hour service offering help to anyone who is in crisis. Helpline: 08457 90 90 90

Youth Access
Offers information, advice and counselling.
Helpline: 020 8772 9900

FOR PARENTS:
ChildLine
45 Folgate Street, London E1 6GL
ChildLine publishes **It hurts me too**, about children's experiences of domestic violence and refuge life.

NCH Action for Children
Charity working with vulnerable children and families needing support. Publishes **The Hidden Victims: Children and Domestic Violence and Making a Difference.**
85 Highbury Park
London N5 1UD
www.nch.org.uk

NSPCC
A charity that runs a free, 24-hour service offering counselling and advice.
National Centre
42 Curtain Road
London EC2A 3NH
Child Protection helpline: 0808 800 5000
www.nspcc.org.uk

Parentline Plus
An organisation offering help, support and information to anyone parenting a child.
Helpline: 0808 800 2222
www.parentlineplus.org.uk

Women's Aid Federation of England
Charity offering support and advice to women and children who have experienced domestic violence.
PO Box 391
Bristol BS99 7WS
Women's Aid domestic violence helpline (free and confidential):
08457 023 468
www.womensaid.org.uk

Index

Picture credits
Front cover (main) Bubbles/Peter Sylent, front cover left to right: Bubbles/Peter Sylent, Bubbles/Jacqui Farrow, Photofusion/Colin Edwards, Bubbles/Chris Rout, 4 Bubbles/Peter Sylent, 5 Bubbles/Angela Hampton, 6 Bubbles/Peter Sylent, 7 Bubbles/Frans Rombout, 8 Corbis/Roy Marsch, 9 Corbis/Tom & Dee Ann McCarthy, 10-11 Bubbles/Angela Hampton, 12 Photofusion/Colin Edwards, 13 Bubbles/Loisjoy Thurstun, 14 Corbis/Walter Smith, 15 Bubbles/Loisjoy Thurstun, 16 Bubbles/Frans Rombout, 17 Bubbles/Loisjoy Thurstun, 18 Bubbles/Denise Hagen, 19 Bubbles/Jacqui Farrow, 20 Bubbles/Peter Sylent, 21 Bubbles/Jacqui Farrow, 22 Bubbles/Chris Rout, 23 Sheila Gray, 24 Corbis/April Saul, 25 Bubbles/Chris Rout, 26 Corbis/Owen Franken, 27 Bubbles/Angela Hampton, 28 Corbis/Jose Luis Pelaez, 29 Bubbles/Angela Hampton, back cover Corbis/Tom & Dee Ann McCarthy